or conceited or proud.
Love is not ill-mannered,
selfish or irritable.
Love does not keep
a record of wrongs.
Love is not happy with evil,
but is happy with the truth.
Love never gives up: its faith,
hope and patience
never fail.

# THE SOURCE
# OF ALL OUR
# STRENGTH

*White Eagle*

THE WHITE EAGLE PUBLISHING TRUST

NEW LANDS · LISS · HAMPSHIRE · ENGLAND

First published November 1996
Second edition November 1999

© Copyright, The White Eagle Publishing Trust,
1996, 1999


British Library Cataloguing-in-Publication Data
A catalogue record for this book is available from the
British Library

ISBN 0–85487–117–9


Set in 11.5 on 12.5 Monotype Spectrum
and printed and bound in Great Britain
at the University Press, Cambridge

# CONTENTS

# FOREWORD

White Eagle has always said that he speaks not
for himself alone, but rather that his words
are inspired by a greater, wise brotherhood at
the next level of life, whose wish and task it is
to help humanity. It is in this spirit that the
selection from his teaching which appears in
this book has been made. Daily life, with its
times of happiness and contentment, as well
as of pressure and responsibility, takes a great
deal of energy and attention for most people.
But for all of us there can be hidden, underly-
ing questions about the meaning of the things
we do and of events in life; and such questions
eventually rise to the surface, particularly

when we come up against a situation which is painful.

In language which is accessible to everyone, White Eagle conveys profound truths about life as a whole: both material life and the greater, spiritual life which underlies it. And within his teaching lie answers to questions which people have been driven to ask down the centuries. The greatest gift which he shares with us is to show the way to freedom, not by renouncing the physical world, but by becoming increasingly aware, as we go about our lives, of our own deep connection with an eternal, spiritual love, power and wisdom—the source of all healing and understanding—which is within each one of us, and is the basis of all life.

We all have a real desire for the qualities of life which sustain us: hope, love, understanding, wisdom, strength and peace. In this spirit, whether your need is for emotional support, for understanding and faith, or for help in dealing with a physical illness, we hope that you will find that this book can touch your heart and bring you peace.

The present volume is a collection of short extracts from White Eagle's teaching, most of which have not been printed before, and which have been chosen specifically for the purpose of seeking to help those who, in whatever way, feel in need of healing, or wish for healing for a loved one or friend. Of course, this truly includes us all.

The sayings, as in their sister volume, THE QUIET MIND, have been arranged in chapters on particular themes, with a short introduction to each. The book is designed to be dipped into at random to allow the thought appropriate to the moment to speak to the heart, but the chapters are also written to follow on, each theme building on the one before, so that White Eagle's words can create a complete picture of how we can increasingly be aware of the real and ever-present source of all our strength.

Whatever your particular need, we hope you will be aware, through White Eagle's words, of the reality of the eternal spirit, in which we are all held, safe, no matter how it sometimes feels.

*

White Eagle lays great importance on the principle of Divine Mother, and on the importance of the feminine aspect in us all—how it is the feminine aspect in each one of us that can lead us most truly to the heart's intuition. Any reader familiar with his teaching will know how he often speaks of the specially important capacity women have to be open and receptive to the energies of the Aquarian Age. Although in some instances he uses masculine words (such as 'brethren' and 'brotherhood') to represent both male and female for ease of speech, we hope that all readers will understand White Eagle's profound respect for the feminine principle. His vision for the new age is one of perfect balance between the so-called 'masculine' and 'feminine' energies.

This second edition includes a number of small revisions, and an extra saying.

# 1

❧

# OPEN YOUR HEART TO GOD

*A great amount of the time our hearts are closed. Not because we want it to be so, but perhaps because we are in pain, or deeply hurt, and cannot understand why life is as it is. Maybe we have temporarily forgotten ourselves and our true values in the helter-skelter of daily living. Whatever the reason for the crust, as White Eagle has called it, around our heart, we have forgotten or find it hard to believe that we are spirit, and that there is an infinite power for good operating throughout all life. In this first section White Eagle helps us to reconnect with the source of our life and happiness, in order to understand and be better able to deal with our daily life.*

## IN TUNE WITH THE INFINITE

If you are sorely troubled, remember there was a time before you became a separate entity in a physical world when you were at one with your Creator on that beautiful level of life in the heaven-world. There you were at one. Down here you are separate. But if you can rise in consciousness and put yourself in tune with the infinite, you will see your problems and difficulties from a very different angle. You will know that all things work together for good, for God, for those who love God. Surrender will then be so simple. All the fret and fear will fall away.

# PART OF GOD

You are part of heaven. You are part of God.
The whole universe is the result of the impulse
of love. God, the supreme mind, the divine
mind, is all love. The main lifestream is love.
Banish all thought of your disability. You, the
spirit, *you* are the son or daughter of a living
God, a power, a divine intelligence; a great, loving, compassionate heart. You live and move
and have your being in the divine mind, the
infinite wisdom.

# TRUE WISDOM

We shall not learn from others or from books,
but find all knowledge within ourselves, for
we are part of all that ever has been and all
that ever shall be…. From the smallest to the

greatest, we partake of all life, because within us is the everlasting God.


## REGAINING CONTROL

If you find it difficult to restrain and control yourselves when you want to, at those moments take a deep breath, and say to yourself many times, 'God is with me'. Then be still and let the all-good manifest through you. You do not *know* how much benefit will come about from this practice.


## YOUR KING IS GOD—IN YOU!

Everything passes, all things change, except God; and God is within you, and is increasing in power. Your consciousness of God is daily increasing, and this is all that matters—the expanding consciousness of God within, who rules your kingdom, the kingdom which is your life.

## THE RAINBOW

A sorrow can be like a rainy day with sunlight shining through. And sun through rain creates a rainbow. So it is with human life. Look to the sunlight of God, knowing that your Father–Mother will send you nothing but good, that your loved ones are in God's care, and that God's love for them is greater than your own.

## GOD TOOK FORM

Do not think of God as a universal power without intelligence, love or personality. Some people deny the existence of a personal, an anthropomorphic God. God took form. God still takes form and comes amongst you and you must look for God in form everywhere in your life. *Seek, and ye shall find.*

## NO BARRIER

Blessed are the pure in heart, the simple ones, who have no barrier between them and this infinite and eternal love ... light, power, Creator.

# 2

꒰◌꒱

# ACCEPTANCE
# OPENS THE DOOR

*When we close our hearts to God, whether consciously, or because of our pain, we are not accepting the central place of spiritual things in our being here; understandably, perhaps, we may not accept the circumstances of our lives, nor that they are an expression of a divine and loving plan for us. Perhaps we are resentful, and struggling to fight what we see as negative.*

*In this section White Eagle talks to us about the power of acceptance, and demonstrates how, in the end, it can transform our lives.*

*The final passage in this chapter was given at Easter.*

## DO YOUR BEST AND THEN ACCEPT

The soul must learn both to accept and to surrender to the almighty Spirit of wisdom and love. Some people will think that surrender means a lying-down, a giving-in to evil; an acceptance of things which should not be. This is not correct. The soul must always strive to do its best in any condition. When you have done your best, then look up to your Creator and surrender to the wisdom and love of the Father–Mother God.

## FORGIVE AND LET GO

You must be wise and you must be strong, but in your strength be kindly and loving towards whatever it is, or whoever it is that has caused you pain.

## ACCEPTANCE BRINGS OPPORTUNITY

We all say, loosely, that karma means a 'paying-off' of debts incurred in a past life; but it is much more, for karma brings opportunity with it. The very act of paying off some karmic debt gives the soul an opportunity to make progress, to step forward.

This is why we say again and again: accept, accept your karma gratefully, even cheerfully. It will seem hard; it is hard, because your lower bodies, including the astral body of desire, and the lower mental body, are clamouring to get their own way, because they do not understand that they are held in God's love. Therefore karma appears hard; but if you can not only accept what you dislike, but realize the opportunity being given you, then in your acceptance and right working-out of that piece of karma, you will grow in consciousness.

## GOD'S WILL, NOT MINE

You have to will that you will the will of God: not only for yourself, but for all life, so that you recognize the omnipotence governing the world, and also governing your own life. You may have an idea that such and such a happening would be just right for you, but in a year's time you may see how wrong it would have been. You can look back upon your life and know that had you had your own way things would have been very different. You have to admit that there is this gentle, guiding hand which is so wise. Had you gone your own way entirely you would never have learned some of the great truths, nor would you have attained any measure of inner peace and spiritual joy.

## BE STILL AND WAIT UPON GOD

If you are in material difficulty and confusion at the present moment, and you do not know what to do, the message is this: be still and wait upon God. But for this you must have faith and humility, so that you will be able to accept what is presented to you as being God's will.

## BE PATIENT

All will work out. All you have to do is to tune in to the right station, the right centre within yourself, and all your problems, heartaches and disappointments will be put right in a far better way than you could imagine. Don't be disappointed … all will come in God's time.

## YOUR OPPORTUNITY WILL COME

You need not rush about to find those things that you can do…. You don't need to 'go' or 'do' until the opportunity is clearly placed before you, and then you will know that you have to act.

## TRULY … ALL IS WELL

So many of you are frustrated in your daily life because things will not go the way you want them to go, and you become very disillusioned with the teaching about God's love.

But we would assure you that as you daily strive to overcome all doubts about the love and wisdom of God, you will be getting nearer and nearer to an expansion of consciousness— the expansion of your own consciousness wherein you will feel, and be blessed with, heavenly joy and comfort and assurance that in God's world all is well.

And what about this world? Is all well for you in this world on the physical plane? Yes, my dears, it is. It is you who are sometimes out of step, not life. You want things to be different from how they are, when what the true aspirant is after is complete acceptance of the wisdom of God's laws.

## ACCEPTANCE MEANS NEW LIFE

Now, as we speak of resurrection, we see the spirit world ablaze with the flowers of Spring, the bursting trees, the running brooks. We hear the orchestra of the little winged creatures. Spring is here! Crucifixion is over and the resurrection come, reborn. This is what we would impress upon you all: after periods of pain and suffering, which you must accept resolutely, look forward to the new life, to the rebirth, which will come in your heart.

# 3

୬

# THE TEMPLE OF YOUR BODY

*White Eagle, who has said, 'You are spirit first and body last', helps us to see that our path of unfoldment is none-theless through physical life: the body, mind and emotions of earth. The body, as temple of the spirit, needs our sup-port and care; it is sacred and beautiful in the eyes of God, since we are created in His—Her image.*

*White Eagle encourages us to see that loveliness in the body; to embrace our earthly life for what it can teach us, and to celebrate all the gifts of life with which we are endowed.*

# ILLUSION

Your physical world is a world of illusion—it is not what you think it is. Do you realize that your physical world, in reality, is a world of light? It is built of light. Do you know that your physical body, if you could see it with clear vision, is composed of light?

# REASON FOR PAIN

The sole purpose of life in the physical body is to develop and unfold the Christ-seed which is planted in the heart of every child of God. All your experiences are intended to bring you deeper understanding. Your sufferings, your loves, your pains, all unfold the rose of Christ within your heart.

# RAISE THE BODY

You are here to use physical matter, and not allow it to dominate you. You are here; you are light; and *you* have to shine out through the darkness. You have to use your physical life and raise it, to transmute the heavy atoms of the physical body.

# BE KIND

Be compassionate and refrain from any condemnation or criticism because these are the emotions which sow seeds of inharmony in the physical body. Remember also not to condemn your own body. Take care, be kind to your brother body, who is your servant and needs your love and your wisdom.

# YOUR LINK WITH THE SPIRITUAL SUN

We trust that those of you who are suffering with some infirmity will take to heart our message, and realize that your true body is a body of solar light…. Look up, and bring through your being that solar force, and may it help you to overcome the little frets and fears and anxieties of your physical body.

## WHEN YOU ARE ANXIOUS

Many of you are confused and anxious, but you should not be so. If you will go into the silence and kneel before your own private altar in the temple of your soul, letting go of all fear, all earthly claims, and becoming as a little child, you will be filled with love. Love for God, love of God: as this love fills your heart

and your mind, then every atom, every cell of
your body, will be filled with perfect life. This
is mastery.

## THE GLORY WITHIN

We would impress upon you the importance
of your life in the physical body. There are
those who think it would be so nice to get out
of the body into the glories of the spirit world.
You will not get into the glories of the spirit
world until you have found these glories
within yourself. You have to learn to realize
these things *in your own being*. This is your golden
world; this is the golden world of God—in the
heart chakra, your own being. And it is not
limited: your consciousness will expand. You
will live in the consciousness of God, and see
the beautiful world of spirit in which you live,

and most of all you will see the sweetness and
love in each human soul.

## THE PERFECT TEMPLE

Life in the physical body should be like the perfect, healthy plant or flower. The flower which
is your life needs to have sufficient nourish-
ment for its roots, its stem, its leaves and its
fruit, and, like any flower, should have its place
in the sunlight, and should live to glorify God.
The body, being the temple of God, should
have recreation, harmony; there should be
opportunities for physical and mental development and interest; opportunities for spiritual culture. All the vehicles contained in
each human being (the physical, etheric, the
astral, mental and celestial) should be growing and expressing the true life of God.

# 4

॰

# FREEDOM FROM
# FEAR AND SUFFERING

*As beings of light in a physical body we have chosen a*
*path of growth, and growth may bring pain as well as joy.*
*Often pain not only arises from, but also feeds, fear. White*
*Eagle helps us to be aware of the choice we constantly*
*have in our lives: whether to think, speak and act out of*
*fear, or out of love. He reminds us of a state of life which*
*can be ours, even now, which is beyond fear and suffering;*
*untouched by it. He helps us to see how through actually*
*living love in our daily lives, and through aspiring to the*

*Great Spirit through meditation, we can release ourselves from the bondage of our sorrow and anxiety.*

## THE PERFECT FLOWER

Father–Mother God does not inflict suffering upon you, but suffering is like the soil of earth into which the seed of life is dropped; and through the changing conditions in the earth and in the elements above the earth, the seed takes root, and in time grows into the perfect flower. Human life is the same.

## THE SEED OF GOD

As within the seed or bulb that you plant in springtime lies the subsequent perfection of form, colour and perfume, so in the seed of God planted in every heart is the promise of the perfect human being. But you see, you yourself have to make the effort; and this is not easy, the effort always to reach up, to believe, and in time to know, that love is the king of life and your saviour.

## USE SUFFERING WISELY

We see so much suffering on earth, and the love which our heavenly Father has given us causes us to long to assuage that suffering. This can only be done by helping our earthly brethren to understand the reason for their suffering, and what suffering can do for them if they accept and use the experience in the right way.

## TRUTH IS LOVE

When you have seen truth within yourself; when you can free yourself of all falsity, and see yourself naked, then the light dawns. As light comes the life changes. You cannot live an untruth. Here then is the central point: truth—and truth is love.

## PRACTISE THE PRESENCE OF CHRIST

To get liberation from the earthly state the individual must practise and live the teaching of Christ—must practise the presence of Christ. By going deep within and being honest with yourself you see this light of truth, and when you know this your life changes; you have started the process of recreation; you have started on the upward arc.

## CONFIDENCE

Rise into the love of God and say, 'Thank you, Father–Mother God, that I have to go through this trial, because it is teaching me to have confidence in your love and your wisdom'.

## THE FUTURE

You all have problems of one kind or another, and many of you have fears for the future.... Never cross your bridge before you come to it. If and when you come to it, you will be carried across it with great power and love.

## NEVER MIND WHAT HAPPENS

You are learning the lesson of patience, and also the lesson of love and constancy. When you have to go through difficulties, hold fast to the law of good. Never mind what happens; and if you are unable to see the reasons for suffering, keep the light burning in your breast, saying again and again: 'God is my Father—

Mother; God is all good, God will bring me safely through'. Do not cling to material things, or even to people—if they go, let them go. If they hurt and disappoint you, that is to teach you—to teach you, maybe, to find your true self. There is only one thing to fear, and that is fear itself. Strive to overcome fear: fear of death, fear of life, fear of loss, fear of suffering. This is the goal: to overcome all fear, and to realize your son–daughtership with the Father–Mother God.

## HAVE COURAGE

Never be afraid. The greatest enemy of humanity is fear. Be confident in the love and the wisdom of God, and remember that if you go into shadow, darkness will not touch you if you are radiating light. Light is love and purity, and all the qualities of the Christ-spirit.

The spirit, the divine spark, will ever rise triumphant over all conditions.

## SURRENDER—DON'T FIGHT

If you are called upon, through your karma, to go through an experience from which you shrink; then if you can resign yourself and surrender wholly and tranquilly to the eternal light—to the pure sweet life of the Lord Christ—and can feel the warmth and the strength and the comfort of that life's all-enfolding love, you will do far better than trying to attack anything which threatens to overwhelm you.

## THERE ARE NO BURDENS

You know, there is an old saying that God strengthens the back to bear the burden. We would assure you that when you see with the eyes of the spirit you will understand a further truth: that there are no burdens except those you yourselves pick up and put on your backs.... We long to show you that you yourselves take burdens upon yourselves. The wise man or woman never does this. They set themselves free to soar in spirit.

## KEEP STEADY AND CALM

When you come up against difficulties and problems do try, dear ones, to remember that these difficulties are testing the strength of your spirit and adding to the stature of your soul. Do not be abashed or disappointed when troubles come along. Be steady, be calm, and if you know the brotherhood law of love you will always know how to deal wisely with the situation.

# FREEDOM

The way to freedom is the way of the Lord
Christ, the Son. It is the way of giving, giving,
giving love. You seek freedom; you seek the
way to free yourselves from the limitation of
the earthly life, of space, of poverty, from the
limitation of all the material conditions of the
world. The way to freedom, which is the goal
of your spirit, is to bring the divine power
within you up and out in service to all humanity. *This* is the way to freedom. The world has
to learn this secret. By giving you are releas-
ing all the creative forces which will return
into your heart with rich treasure.

# GOD IS IN THE UNKNOWN

It is natural for you all to fear the unknown,
but you can be quite sure that God is in the

unknown, and has His–Her own way of providing for every child in creation. In every case, without exception, God has magic to shed upon your lives and upon your experiences. The wise man or woman confidently puts their hand in the hand of their Master and resolutely refuses to be frightened about anything. They know that God is there, God is with them, and His angels have their wings about them. If you would resign yourself to God in trust, you would know the most beautiful peace, and light would fill your soul.

# 5

❧

# A BALANCED LIFE

*A balance is created when the earthly self knows itself to be in tune with the spiritual purpose of life, and seeks to act from this spiritual centre. White Eagle helps us to find this way of being, which he refers to as poise. When we read his words we are led to the calm centre of things, where we know that all is well, no matter what is happening around us.*

*Central to this way of living is knowing the importance of the whole or holy breath—consciously breathing in the spirit, and breathing out love. Practising this, we thereby create harmony in our nervous system, and in our whole being.*

## RELEASE YOURSELF

We in spirit do not give names to disturbances in the physical body. We are concerned with creating harmony in the body—creating ease, relaxation, a purity of thought, which loosens all the knots, at the etheric level, and then at the physical level wherever the disturbance lies. Concentrate on the harmony of the soul.

Joy in life is so important to you. There is no need to attack problems: just bring this harmony into life, and do not think of earth and heaven as separate. Think of the interpenetration, the radiation, of that supreme creative light.

# THE INNER HARMONY

If you learn to listen to the inner harmony within your heart, you will know that you are enfolded by a company of shining sons and daughters of God. They reach down to help you that are younger to rise in spirit into that eternal world of love and perfect brotherhood.

# THE GRAPH GOES UP AND DOWN

On this path the graph goes up and down. The soul is bound to be carried up to the heights and bound to descend again. At times you will feel full of spiritual ecstasy and can do anything; and there will be times when you feel hopeless. Never, *never* mind. Hold on with a loving heart to your ideal, and to your Father—Mother God, who understands you, thereby bringing the light within into conscious operation, so that the very cells of your body become finer.

## LET NOTHING DISTURB YOU

All of you have to learn to gain knowledge, and it is the actual experience of living with your companions which enables you to gain wisdom. Wisdom says that bitter and painful experiences grow more painful if you allow them to disturb you emotionally and mentally. We all have to learn to lay them on one side: have to learn to forget everything except the love of the Son of God.

## ASPIRATION BRINGS CONTROL

When you fail to control passion, or to control your thoughts and emotions, you cause a hold-up in your spiritual circulation. So strive for control, not so much by sheer will-power, but by aspiring continually in everyday life to touch the pure and holy planes of life.

## BALANCING THE ELEMENTS

The purpose of spiritual unfoldment is to bring harmony into the whole being so that all planes of consciousness are harmonized in the one supreme light, which contains, shall we say, the seven rays or the seven colours of the spectrum. That light is the pure Christ light. Aspire to that, so that you reach the centre of truth, and your contact will be complete and whole, and from it will come powers of expansion and development.

## FAITH EVEN IN THE DARKNESS

When the soul has received a certain amount

of illumination and been caught up into the heavens, it is all the more bitter to come down and remain on earth.

The thing to do then is to learn to accept that condition patiently. You may have this experience often or infrequently. These periods usually follow a time of great exultation, when you have felt, 'Now I know truth, life will always be different!' But there will be periods when your soul is going through the dark night. Once you learn to accept that condition tranquilly as being part of your growing, part of the divine plan, something arises in you which we will call the 'lesser light' to illumine your path.

If you become agitated then you will not learn the lesson which the condition is intended to teach you. The 'lesser light' is your confidence and faith, and teaches you to be still, to be patient, and not to force the issue.

# JOY IN SUFFERING

With clearer vision you would see how all human life works for harmony; how it is working all the time to develop in the soul a state of harmony and freedom from bondage by the earthly self, by the mind of earth.

You see, karma is nothing to shrink from, dear ones, but something to rejoice in, even if it brings discomfort. All growth is apt to seem an uncomfortable process, and birth also can be uncomfortable; but see what it leads to in the end!


# BREATHE IN THE QUALITIES OF GOD

Consider the act of breathing, breathing the holy breath—not only of air but of life, God's life: God's light ... love ... health ... vitality

... God's beauty and wisdom. Do this, with the feeling that you are being revivified and revitalized through your whole being. We remind you most truly that breathing can be an act of holiness. Holiness means healthfulness. So, when you are conscious of the inhalation of God you are healing your body and soul and revivifying your spirit.... The holy breath brings to your consciousness harmony, the harmony of the spiritual spheres.

## OPEN THE WINDOWS OF YOUR SOUL

May every day of life find you, when you rise in the morning, opening the windows of your soul to the sunlight. Even in Winter the whole atmosphere is impregnated with tiny atoms of invisible sunlight, and when you breathe deeply, consciously breathing in the sunlight of God, you grow in wellbeing; in loving kindness to all life; and also you will begin to become aware of the power of the invisible forces which you may contact. You must learn how to open yourself to the sunlight and how to purify your body, so that you may contact the angelic influences.

# 6

೩

# TOLERANCE AND
# FORGIVENESS

*A feeling of harmony and poise brings with it the ability
to understand and to be tolerant towards others. White Eagle
shares with us the importance of this kindness and tender-
ness in our dealings with others, and how we can let go
enough to do this. He also reminds us of how important it
is to forgive—not only to forgive others, but also to forgive
ourselves for the times we seem to fail. He brings closer to
us the feeling of the Master's love—the sweet, gentle love
in which we are all held, without any condemnation. If we*

*could really believe in that love for us, White Eagle says, perhaps we could more readily show it in our dealings with others.*

## FORGIVE YOURSELF

Jesus so frequently said to those who were healed: *Go thou and sin no more.* He enfolded them in divine forgiveness and love. This is the core of the healing magic. Forgiveness arises from the Christ light deep within your own heart. 'Forgive yourself as I forgive you', says the Master. Deep, deep healing rises from the heart of the child of God, and its source is love.

## DIVINE LAW

You cannot hurt any living thing without hurting yourself, and the whole of life. Every tear you dry, every pain you remove from another, comes back to you in blessing.

## A KINDLY THOUGHT

You do not need a lot of dogma or creeds—just a kindly thought, or kindly word, and a realization that however difficult your brother or sister may be they are striving, though unconsciously, to reach that highest level of consciousness ... and you will find what is called a reward in your complete joy and peace and happiness in life.

## HOLD THE STAR IN YOUR HEART

These are the qualities of a great soul: gentleness and tolerance. You all think you know best. You all think the other person is doing the wrong thing. Tolerance, tolerance, dear ones. Live and let live. Let everybody have the freedom they need in order to grow and develop. Your work is to hold in your heart the shining star, which is all love, and stillness and strength.

## GIVE ALL

Give all the love, all the light that you have within you. Give it all. Broadcast it every moment of your life: in problems with your family, problems with your companions, the answer is to give and give and give that simple light, that pure light of the Son of God which is in your heart. So simple, but so difficult.

## NEVER DESPAIR

One thing we beseech you not to do, is to give up hope because you think you are so futile, so unworthy. Know your failings and your weaknesses, but have courage, for every effort that you put forth is a spark of light. If you have what you call failure, do not despair and say, 'I am not there yet'. The very fact that you are trying shows you are there. If not, you would not be trying.


## BEING SORRY

Everything is recorded on the Akashic register, but there are certain things that you would prefer not to be recorded, and you hope that you can rub out. Well you can, you can, dear ones: by that great love of God, you can be sorry, and by being sorry and trying to eradicate your fault, you do eradicate it, and the record is wiped away. But the record of all that is good is there!

# LET GO GUILT

It is a temptation for you to hug to yourself a sense of guilt for past errors—this may even come from a previous incarnation. You may feel truly humble, seeking purification; but do not, we ask you, retain any sense of guilt for past errors. Look into the love of God, the boundless mercy of God. Give yourselves in loving submission to your Creator, and you will be filled with divine love.

## KARMA AND FORGIVENESS

Karma can most certainly be transmuted by the Christ light, and the Christ light is the forgiving heart. In forgiveness lies the secret of transmutation of karma. *Forgive us our trespasses, as we forgive....* Always that loving spirit, that desire to forgive: to forgive means that you are forgiven. We would remind you that karma is also an opportunity, because it is through what you would, perhaps erroneously, call bad karma that you gain wisdom. The karma which you have to work out in your physical life can be the greatest gift to you in helping you to rise.

## A JEWEL IN YOUR TEMPLE

The great lord of karma rules your ways. Apparent injustice can be turned into a jewel in your temple, and some of the deepest sufferings have brought the divinest truths. So let us do away with this sense of injury, and look out upon the world with a calm love.

## WHEN YOU FALL

Your guardian angel has seen you fall and does not condemn; does not say, 'There, I told you so!'—but would whisper in your heart, 'Courage.... Let us raise you again'.

# 7

❧

## LOVE HEALS

*In this section, we come to the heart of the teaching which White Eagle brings through for us—that love is the greatest power there is.*

*Love, which is pure wisdom and creative power, can overcome all limitation and resistance, and set us free. It is the true healing power, and White Eagle helps us to feel this love flowing to us from the spirit, but also shows us how to connect with it in our daily lives with others in order to heal our relationships.*

## LOVE IS THE KEY

This is the true secret of all healing: seek for harmony in your human relationships. Love all your fellow men and women, love all creatures. Feel in your heart that gentleness of the Masters. Love, and your whole body will be recreated. It will shine with the light of heaven. The healing power is the power which is released by love.

## THE CRUCIFIXION OF THE SELF

Selfishness cuts you off from the heavenly world. The lower self holds you down to physical matter, but by right living and right thinking, by aspiration and often by way of crucifixion, you can find your way to the heavenly state, and once there you know you find truth. In this way you find truth through love.

# THE BOOMERANG!

Your actions, your whole life, make a vibration, or a sound. Every individual soul is therefore sounding a note, a vibration. When the harmonious and right vibration goes forth from you it finds its exact mark, and so it will return. As you sound, so you will receive; this is cause and effect.

This happens on all planes: spiritually, when you send out that note of Christ love, you naturally absorb into yourself harmony, peace of mind, all things which create in your environment harmony and progress. It is an exact law. On the physical plane, as you sound the right note, you will find disease will disappear: you will become healthy.

## BE LOVE

Go about the world *being* love, being caring,

not only to those who are congenial to you, but to all men and women. Do not fall into the error of regarding anyone at all as your enemy. No man or woman is your enemy, all are your teachers.

## NO CONDEMNATION

To be healthy is to be holy. Holy means to be whole, perfect. To be perfect means seeing imperfection with the eyes of the Master: the eyes of loving understanding and acceptance. Strive for tolerance. Never condemn your brother or sister—love them.

## YOU CAN LOVE

Many of you have said to us, 'My heart is like a stone. I have not got any feeling. I cannot love'.

This is not really so. It is only just a crust which has to be broken through. The fire is in everyone's heart.

What you will find helpful is to cultivate tolerance and patience. Remember the difficulties which confront the other soul; the limitations which it is feeling. But first and foremost your need is to make contact with the Christ love. Get above personalities to the divine heart, and that light flowing into you will bring you warmth. You won't have the emotionalism which earth people think is love, but something superior … a light, a gentleness, a sweetness, a kindness without words, will flow from you. That is *real* love.

## GOOD ABSORBS EVIL

In all creation there are the two aspects: the unevolved aspect, and the aspect which is slowly evolving; the negative side of life, and the positive side, which is positive good. The positive good absorbs what you call evil. In other words, positive good is all love, which enfolds what is called evil, absorbs it into itself, and from it creates good.

## TURN YOUR THOUGHTS AROUND

You live in a shell, endeavouring to hide from others your feelings, and even the light which is your true self. Therefore you, who look at your brothers and sisters from the outside of life, can never see the real self beneath the covering of materiality and mortality. We say to you that in every human heart there is something to love. When you are tempted to say of another, 'Oh how selfish he or she is; how greedy; how unkind!', turn those words about and say instead: 'How good he is, how well she means ... they are doing their best'. As you look for the best in everyone, in spite of the mists which obscure it, so strength will flow into you, and peace will dwell in you.

## TO ACHIEVE LOVE

May we just suggest that when you find it difficult, or almost impossible, to love an individual, you forget all the little human failings and weaknesses in them which make it so difficult for you to love, and just give your heart to the Perfect One—to Him who commanded the waters to be still? Let the Perfect One live as an image in your heart, and you will be flooded with light. You will have no difficulty then in feeling an immense love. The personalities will change; they will become very dear to you. This is one way to achieve love.

# MISUNDERSTANDING

Now, even on earth, when there are little misunderstandings which crop up with your brother, sister, husband, wife, whatever relative or friend it is—a little friction, only a misunderstanding of communication—try to be sorry; try and overcome in yourself that little misunderstanding. And you can do this, dear ones, if you remember the love in which you were born; the love by which you live; the love which is flowing to you from nature; the love which sustains you, body and soul.

Remember the love which protects you in your daily life, which will never, *never* fail you; which will always guide you on to the path of righteousness, or rightness—the right path. We know the joy and the happiness which can fill the human life when this truth is understood.

## BE READY FOR JOY

What a joy to feel the quality of love in others! The little things which irritate the outer mind and the little self, let them fall from you … and see in each of your companions this beautiful spirit of love and service which you yourself would have. Go forth to love, and instantly notice the need of your brother, your sister: be ready with a work of love and helpfulness.

## LIVING LOVE

You cannot know yourself with all your earthly thinking; you can only know yourself through your spiritual awakening and subsequent study and meditation, and by practising the presence of God. This practising the presence of God is the hardest thing in the world. Jesus came in all simplicity and humility to say: *Love one another.* But it is hard for you to love all beings. Can you though for a moment conceive what life might be if all people loved one another and practised the presence of God?

# 8

### 🕊

# THE TRANSFORMING POWER

*Because love sets us free, and can overcome all negativity, it is the greatest and most potent force, but it is a force which is gentle, kind and peaceable. This is divine power.*

*White Eagle helps us to realize the true source of our strength and wellbeing, and also how, when we turn the other cheek, and aspire to God, we open the door to an incalculable power for good, and for healing, simply because we have put ourselves in harmony with the immense creative force behind all life—divine love.*

# THE PILLARS OF PROTECTION

You pray; you sometimes cry out in your need to your protector—the Great White Spirit—which is the canopy of your temple. But, in order for you to receive full protection, you need to develop within yourselves qualities of the spirit which are like the pillars supporting the canopy. This means that when in daily life these Christlike qualities are put into operation, then by spiritual law, all the protection, the guidance, the help that a soul needs comes to it.

## ALL NEED IS MET

As you give yourselves in service, so is your life-force being replenished. There is no end to the life-force; it moves in a circle. There is no beginning and no end to life—it is eternal.

## PRAYER IS POWERFUL

As a soul seeks truth by silent prayer it receives a great power, not that which urges domination over any other soul, but power to live graciously, beautifully; a power to transmute the earthly atoms to a higher form.

## A WELL-OILED MACHINE

If your foundation-stone of love is not secure, then no matter what you do with your mortal minds in the way of organization and direction, it will not help. Never mind if things are not what your mortal minds would have them. There is a power working behind all form and it will work through you much more readily if you give conditions for it to flow. If you put the spiritual, loving, gentle things first, everything must then work like a well-oiled machine!

# THE DIVINE POWER AWAKES

When you become storm-tossed by fear, anxiety and passion, the divine power, the force which should control you, is sleeping.... You call, in your daily lives, 'I am afraid'. Everything is tumbling around you. The boat of your soul rocks in a great storm. When the soul calls rightly the Master hears. In you rises the divine power which causes you to be still, to be tranquil. Be at peace.

# HOW TO COPE

There is no need to worry about anything. You are governed in life by spiritual laws. God knows your need. If certain experiences are coming they are sent to you through the wisdom of God. There is no need to be anxious.

Hold up your head and square your shoulders, and say, 'This is going to help me, not destroy me'.

## YOU WILL NOT KNOW TIREDNESS

If you will meditate upon the presence of the beautiful Christ-spirit you will absorb the essence of the Christ being, the essence, or perfume, which will quicken your own bodily vibration so that all tiredness and heaviness depart. You will not know tiredness when you come to the edge of the aura of the Great One.

## SENSITIVITY

As you progress on the spiritual path you are also increasing your sensitivity. The nervous system becomes very sensitive. It is like walking a razor edge, for on the one hand you need to develop this sensitivity, because this quality enables you to receive heavenly guidance and comfort, and help in your daily life; but, at the same time, you also have to develop the inner power of God, which brings tranquillity. This power of God is love.

## TRUE AS STEEL

Out of all your current experiences on earth there will presently come something worthwhile, something true as steel, something perfect and wholly good. It is therefore worth the effort you are making to live and to aspire to God. You are returning in full consciousness and glory and power to your Creator.

# 9

❧

# NO DEATH

*Such divine power of love as the sayings in the last section
have described overcomes all sickness and inharmony, and
eventually can recreate all the cells of the physical body.
One day the physical form itself will become so spiritualized
that there will no longer be any death of the body. But,
even now, although the body dies, we do not.*

*This is one of the central messages of White Eagle's
teaching, and again and again he asks us to remember this
and let it influence our beliefs. We have no need to fear.
We will not even know the moment of our death, but we*

*will be met by those we love who have gone before. For our true home, White Eagle reassures us, is in the world of light, and the more we learn to touch that world of spirit while we are still in a physical form, the more we will know for certain that life is eternal.*

## INTO A WORLD OF BEAUTY

Death is not a dark vale. Death is the most beautiful passage opening into a world of beauty. For you will not know when you take your last breath. You will be entirely unconscious that it is your last breath, but you will feel you are lighter—you are free!

## AN AWAKENING

Why do you fear, my children? You have nothing to fear except your own fear. What is death but a sleeping and very often a forgetting of earthly life; an awakening to a life more radiant and more harmonious?

## YOU ARE ETERNAL

You are eternal, and as you are today so you will be tomorrow. As you create yourself, and build the spiritual atoms into your soul, you will be able to enjoy the fruits which the Lord has prepared for you in the higher state of life. The world of spiritual life is not geographically far away from you. It is within you; it is within your own consciousness … the higher worlds, the light worlds are instantly to be found when you open yourself in love.

## LIFE AND DEATH ARE ONE

Dismiss from your mind any idea of 'here' and 'there', of earth and heaven. Conceive of life as one eternal whole. By learning spiritual law and by putting it into operation in your daily life, you can then commence to taste the fruits of heaven; you will commence to grow in spirit and in awareness of life invisible. You will then no longer regard death as something either to dread, or to welcome (as some people may). You will know that death changes you not at all.

## INITIATION

What you call death is truly an initiation. The soul goes forth, not to lose its identity, but to gain greater consciousness of God, and of the eternal light.

## NO DIFFERENCE

It is true; there is no death. When you have

passed the great barrier you will be amazed and say, 'But I did not feel anything! Am I dead? I feel exactly the same'. There is no difference, except that you have taken off one set of clothes and left it behind; you are no longer interested in it. That is all that death means.

## DEATH IS A
## BEAUTIFUL EXPERIENCE

However you pass away from your physical body, whether it is by an accident, or a sudden passing, or whether it is a slow process of withdrawing from physical matter, we would like you to understand that God is with you, and God is all love. The withdrawal—even the shock of a sudden death in war, or by accident—is *always* a beautiful experience for the soul.

# YOU CANNOT DIE

When you are in meditation, in a flash of illumination you may touch that level of cosmic consciousness. Then you will surely know that life is eternal, and that life has always been and always will be, and that you are that life. You cannot die; you will never die. Life changes form, but it never dies.

# THE ETERNAL NOW

It is a mistake always to think in terms of the future. Many people live out their lives in this fashion. They say, 'If only so and so would happen I should be perfectly happy'. But this is wrong. It is in the eternal now that you have to live, and realize your at-one-ment with God.

# EXPAND YOUR VISION

It is time for you to be completely convinced that there is no obliteration such as death—that your life goes on. But more than this, you have to get firmly into your mind that you have, within you *now*, capacity to expand your vision, your being, your activity, on to higher and wider planes of life.

## AT THE ACCEPTABLE
## TIME OF THE LORD

Be patient, dear ones, when you have to hold the hand of a loved one passing from one plane to another. The process of birth cannot be hurried. You can only wait. A great deal is going on in preparing that soul; in adjusting it for its beautiful birth into the spirit world ... and always remember that there is a love and wis-

dom far greater than your own taking care of
that soul.

## WALK IN THE ETERNAL GARDEN

If you are heart-sad, you will be comforted.
*Blessed are they that mourn.* Know that you can
never be separated from your own loved ones.

Death, as you know it, does not separate.
You crave for the physical form. Crave, instead,
for the spirit. Communicate with the spirit.
Think of the infinite and eternal garden. Walk
in that garden. When you go to sleep at night
let your last thought be of praise and thank-
fulness to God. Think of the world of light and
crossing the river to the other side. Direct
yourself by the divine will that is within you.
Let it be your director in your sleep and in your
waking.

# THE FLAME OF LIFE ETERNAL

Let the symbol of the Holy Grail and the little flame remind you that this is the light in your own heart—the light, the divine essence of life, the infinite and eternal love. There is no death. The body falls away as an old dress, but the spirit, which is the Son of God, can never, never die.

# 10

❧

# THE GREAT HEALER

*Jesus, the Great Healer, demonstrated the power of selfless love to overcome death of the physical body, and to bring true healing to others. White Eagle tells us that Jesus is at the head of the healing ray, and that all the healing brotherhood 'of angels and of men and women' work under Him to bring order out of chaos; relief from pain and suffering; and calm to the tumultuous emotions.*

*If we open our hearts to His love we will be blessed with deep peace and understanding. White Eagle helps us to know that we can find the Great Healer ourselves, in our hearts, whenever we sound the password of love, and humbly ask.*

## THE CHRIST IS WITH
## YOU AND WITHIN YOU

For those who are sick, and suffering, just attune yourselves to the perfect and glorious Christ presence.... The Christ presence is *here*.... If you centre all your thoughts upon the Christ presence you may feel the touch. You may feel it upon your head or your shoulders, or your hands, or you will feel the warm, golden light of Christ pouring right through your body, animating, resuscitating all the atoms which are sick and weary.

## DIGNITY AND HOPE

Above all is the supreme grand Master—the Golden One—the Lord Christ. Although you feel that you are insignificant, you are not missed, you are not passed over by the Christ. The Golden One knows you. We want you to remember, think and feel the dignity of your life: what you are, and what you can become.

## RISE UP

What did Jesus say to all those he healed? 'Take up your bed and walk.' 'Rise up and walk.' He took the hand of the little daughter of Jairus and said, 'Rise, little one, wake up'. He says to you, 'Rise, wake up to the living glory of the spiritual world!'

## THE WISDOM OF THE FATHER IS YOURS

Forget your body and your lower mind, and concentrate on the centre of light within your being.... It is like an immense Sun, or circle of radiant light ... most delicate; glowing with all the soft radiance of the spiritual heart of life. Now see, coming into your vision, the form of the simple, loving Master, the embodiment of the Cosmic Christ. Can you feel and respond to the Master's blessing? Do you feel the enfoldment of this love? The gentle Master knows and will give you the wisdom to act rightly.

## GENTLE STRENGTH

We hold before you the life of the Master Jesus—such a simple, pure, holy life. But it was a remarkable demonstration of how life can be lived in the physical body; a life of sacrifice and service, a life of love, but a life also requiring firmness and strength. Don't think that love means you always have to be easy-going and soft. There are times when you have to grip a situation with courage and determination, and with trust and faith in the Great Spirit.

## OUR FRIEND

We give this message to everyone who will accept it: *have no fear.* Just confide in your heart to your gentle brother Jesus, who will come very close to you, closer than breathing, closer than any of your loved ones in a physical body, and He will say to you, 'Remember that we are one with the heavenly Father; be strengthened, for the Lord thy God is with thee'.

## THE FRAGRANCE OF THE ROSE

Your deep need, dear children, is to be able, at all times, to catch the voice of the Master of Love across the oceans of turmoil and conflict;

to feel and inhale the beauty and the fragrance of His aura.

# 11

❧

# MIRACLES HAPPEN CONSTANTLY

*White Eagle reassures us that because life is governed by the laws of love, as well as karma, so miracles are happening in our lives all the time, often without us being aware of them.*

*Along with the healing brotherhood, the Masters are constantly at work on the etheric planes bringing to the earth light where there is darkness, and keeping the development of humanity on course. And miracles can happen for us in our daily lives, too, if we turn our faces to the light of the spirit, and our thoughts towards wholeness, holiness and healthfulness—towards God.*

## THE HEALING
## POWER OF CHRIST

Spiritual healing comes about by the power of spiritual aspiration. When the thoughts are truly aspiring to the Christ, then the light of Christ—the rays of Christ—falls into the heart; and as soon as the rays of Christ are felt in the physical body, having great power they can reverse the order of things. Where there was dark showing in the physical body, they reverse the order to light and the light takes possession, dominating the body and controlling the physical atoms. This is how miracles are performed.

# THE HIDDEN BLESSING

A miracle is a happening which is beyond human understanding, but only because it is outside known physical laws. We are sure that if you look for miracles you will be surprised to find they are continually happening. If you truly look you will be able to recognize the miracles which are happening every moment all around you.... Behind every difficulty there is a hidden blessing.

# YOU CAN SPEED THE MIRACLE

The healing ray works slowly, but surely. But as each one of you will accept and respond to the love of God, giving love yourself, then that speeds it, accentuates the healing miracle. And if you are one of those who have asked for a miracle to happen to you, and it has not happened, remember what we tell you: though you cannot see the miracle, the miracle has happened, not yet to your body, maybe, but certainly to your soul.

## DIVINE WILL

No disease is incurable, but, at the same time, the cure of that disease rests not upon the healer, but upon the will of the patient, and upon the will of God.

## SURRENDER TO GOD'S WILL

You have to develop the consciousness of the power of the star to perform miracles. But remember it is not your will when a miracle is performed. It is God's power; it is God's will. God is the light in the human being, and God alone gives or withdraws according to divine wisdom. We hope you understand that, and will not force what you think ought to be done. Surrender, my children, surrender to God's will in all things.

## ALL ARE PERFECT

All are perfect in God's mind. You on earth only see imperfection, but in the higher spheres the brethren see perfection; they see the children of God as they truly are, and as they will recreate their own lives and souls in time.

## TRANSFORMATION

Spiritual healing cannot fail. It never fails, although it may look to you as though it has failed because the physical body has been unable, because of its karma, to be reborn. The time has come for the soul to be released, but the body into which it is released is perfect. Think of the change from the little grub into the beautiful butterfly, or the lovely dragon-fly!

## THE POINT WITHIN THE CIRCLE

Live in the unwavering consciousness that with God ... good ... love ... all things are possible. God is within your innermost being, and if only you will train yourselves to realize this, that you are the point within the circle of God, you are the point within the blazing Star, then you will find deep peace in your heart.

# 12

❧

# THINK WELL, RELAX, BE WELL

*In the following passages White Eagle helps us to realize just how powerful our thoughts are in the healing process. He shows us how to use the creative power of thought for good, both for ourselves and for others, and describes for us the effect of our thought upon the health and wellbeing of the body, and of the world as a whole. It may be hard for us to realize just how much we can do, through changing the way we think, but White Eagle helps us to understand the importance and wisdom of concentrating on good, beauty, hope and joy, in order to bring these qualities into our lives. This positive attitude of mind brings peace, and helps us truly to relax.*

## GOOD THOUGHT—GOD THOUGHT

Those people who are positive that God is love, and that they must develop the God light within them, receive inspiration. So you see the necessity for always keeping your thoughts pure and your speech good and positive, because the spiritual law says that like attracts like. Positive thoughts of health and holiness attract health and holiness, or wholeness.

## YOU WILL TRIUMPH

Do not admit failure. Deny negative things. Admit only achievement, triumph, and your body will respond. Every particle, every cell of your body is subject to the divine power and glory. The real you, the Christ within you, reigns supreme.

## A SIMPLE CHILD

The intellect can be an enemy, but when properly trained can be your friend. For you to become in tune with the infinite, pride and arrogance of the outer mind must fall away. Blessed are the simple and the pure in heart, for they shall see God. Truly great is the one who can become as simple as a child in the presence of God.

## LOOK UP

Look up ... up into the mountain heights. From the great Star circle there is a radiation extending for an immense distance. This radiation descends to earth not only as wisdom, knowledge and divine intelligence, but also as inspiration and good thoughts: loving, gentle thoughts, which urge you to do kind actions to others, and yourself; to control and discipline all the hastes of your outer life.

## GOD UPHOLDS THE WORLD

You are all tense, and it is for your good and your health and your peace of mind consciously to practise relaxation. If you will endeavour to get the feeling that the world is holding you up instead of you holding the world up, you will be surprised how much easier you feel. You cannot hold the world up, God does that. And God upholds you.

## THE OCEAN OF PEACE

Relax, be still. There is nothing to fear. You must try each day to relax. Let yourself float in the ocean of infinite love. Be still and know God. Just rest, feel that you are sustained on a great ocean of strength and of infinite peace. Your needs are all known to invisible and angelic presences, and every true need will be met. Have confidence in the source of your life. Be still; all is well.

## THE WAY THAT YOU DO IT

You feel you have too much to do; but you know, it is not the amount of work, it is the way you do it that causes you to be battered and worn out; it is your attitude of mind towards that work. If you are interested and put the God within you into whatever you are doing in that moment; if you do one thing at a time quietly, and do not have a million other things in your mind at the same time, then you will find that you will get through all the work you have to do quite calmly, and you will feel refreshed instead of worn out at the end of the day.

## LET GO COMPLETELY

If you have a period of relaxation, completely relax your body and your mind and give yourself up to the revivifying spiritual forces. Enjoy your rest, be filled with sunlight, enjoy nature, lie upon Mother Earth, and absorb the magnetism of the earth. Breathe in the air and glorify in it. Use periods of relaxation wisely and healthfully.

# THE WHITE MAGIC WHICH HEALS

Don't let the mind block your way—follow the inner light, the universal love. This is what Christ is—the universal love which the heavenly Father and Mother have placed in your heart. Jesus said: *I am the light of the world.* The I AM is the seed of God in the heart; it is the light; it is the still, small voice which speaks in every human heart; it is the white magic which heals, which brings order and happiness out of chaos and sorrow.

# 13

❧

# FOLLOW THE LIGHT WITHIN

*When we dwell on thoughts of God we are turning towards the inner light, the Christ light and power within our own heart, the seed of God in human form. If we endeavour to follow that light constantly, we will, White Eagle says, be allowing the magic of the Christ to work for us, and our lives will flow more smoothly. He helps us to believe, also, that each one of us, whatever we are inclined to believe about ourselves, does have that light within—that spirit, which is ever there to guide and to uphold us if we will turn to it.*

# RECREATE YOUR LIFE

We remind you that the light of Christ is in you, in your heart. Become, as Jesus advised you to become, as little children; simple, trusting and believing, because the little voice within you will urge you to believe that God is the source of your life. And as soon as you can come into communion with that power, you are being recreated.


# THE COMING OF THE KINGDOM

We all desire the kingdom of heaven to come on earth, not only for our own happiness, but for the wellbeing and happiness of all creatures. Do not look outside; look inside and see the way. Look into the mirror. Look into the mirror honestly, quietly, in silence, and say, 'I will be God's son–daughter'.

# WHICH PATH ARE YOU TAKING?

Your feelings must be slowly developed from desire for self-preservation to love for God and all God's creation. Be aware, now, of these two forces, ignorance and knowledge, physical matter and spiritual life, and decide which path you are taking. Are you yearning to learn and to understand the meaning of the path, the meaning of the light? Are you following the path of the spirit?

# YOU ARE SPIRIT FIRST

Get it firmly fixed in your mind and do not allow the doubts to creep in: you have a soul and spirit as well as a body. Therefore get it firmly established in your consciousness that you are primarily spirit, and not body. Act by the spirit; let goodness and love always be your guide, no matter what your circumstances and conditions. You cannot go wrong if you follow the true inner light which is the voice of God—of Christ.

## POISE

You are here to learn wisdom. Your heart is full, it is loving, but that is not enough by itself. You must strive for poise, inner strength and wisdom.

## DEVELOP INNER WISDOM

The intuition has to be developed. Mistakes do not matter. In comparison with the greater and wiser ones we all make mistakes. Certainly, therefore, it is right to strive to develop the intuition, but make sure that the inner voice comes from the heart of wisdom, and not from the self that wants something, the desire self. Intuition comes like a flash—it is an inward knowing. The necessity is to have courage to act on it; to be prepared for whatever it brings. The intuition can be developed in meditation, through quiet contemplation within the sanctuary of the heart.

## GREATER PRECISION

People think that by turning their attention to spiritual matters they will get nothing accomplished. This is not true. By strengthening the spirit within you, you will find yourselves living with greater precision. Your powers of execution will grow more perfect than when you allow yourself to be swallowed up in confusion and chaos.

## BEAUTY AND PEACE

Dear ones of earth, the beauty that awaits you is there now; it is only for you to raise your thoughts and humbly believe in God's love and divine will for your complete perfection. May this beauty and this peace be ever present in your hearts.

## ATTUNE TO THE LIGHT

When you open yourself to the inner light, it begins to iron away all the creases of the physical body. People grow old because of the emotions, the anxieties, the worries they permit to come to them. Why do people grow sick? Because of emotional stress and strain—overstraining of the body. If you were always attuned to the Great White Light, there would be no sickness.

# 14

୬

# THE POWER OF
# THE SILENCE

*In order to be truly aware of that inner guidance and power of the Christ, we need, as White Eagle tells us in the following passages, to be able to enter the silence of our hearts; to lay aside the earth for a while and withdraw into the stillness and quiet of the inner world of spirit in meditation, prayer and contemplation. We need to learn how to make times in our lives to do this, and also to be silent within, free of our own thoughts, when we are listening to others. Through the silence we touch the power of the spirit, and we truly create an empty grail cup which can then be filled with the word of God.*

## THE GREAT SILENCE

Those who are accustomed to meditate will know that at a certain point you can touch the great silence, the centre, the source of all good, the most ancient of symbols of which is the dot within the circle—the Christ. To pray is to touch the timeless, eternal centre and this has the most powerful effect both on yourself and those around you.

## TOUCH THE SILENCE

When you are distracted by material things, keep very calm, keep very still. Remember the Brethren of the Silence, whose very power of achievement lies in silence. Touch the silence, and the power of the spirit will flow into you and disperse all your fears.

## THE INNER SANCTUARY

Always remember in the silence of the inner sanctuary your true nature and the use that you can be to God, to the angels and to humanity, in being a ready vessel for the incoming of the light.... Breathe it in.... Become light! Arise into the light of your true self.

## MISTAKES

You make mistakes. Of course every soul in physical life makes mistakes; in the process of learning, mistakes and errors are made, but you will not make so many mistakes if you keep silent. Do not speak; do not rush forward. If you rush forward you can only be hurt and may hurt another. Be patient and be silent, and above all fill your heart with love.


## NO HURRY

Spiritual healing power works silently. It does not rush. God never hurries.


## THE PLACE OF THE SILENCE

Strive to find the place of utter silence deep, deep within yourself. It lies beneath all thought or thinking. It is not to be arrived at through any process of mental concentration: it is a sweet, simple awareness of the divine light. It *is* the inner master, the true teacher.

# EVERYDAY MEDITATION

My dear ones, enter the silence. Be still for a short time every day.... Whenever you can, withdraw from the crowd, and seek contact with that divine life, which you will recognize in yourself as a vibration or feeling of peace, of love, and of great light. You can carry that light in your heart as you go amid the crowds.

# TOGETHERNESS

It is not necessary to draw apart from your brother or your sister, for within yourself is the sanctuary ... in the desert you may experience the tumult and storm of fear and anxiety; and in the great city you may yet walk the streets in perfect peace—poise of spirit—placid and still.

# NO MAN CAN LIVE FOR HIMSELF

You must learn to be still and listen to God's voice, which is showing you that all are one in spirit. When you are released from your prison of flesh (or the mental mind) you will know this vital truth: that you cannot live for yourself alone. You may at times feel bereft and lonely, but the purpose of your life is to enable you to work with your Creator—to develop in yourself the wisdom of how to commune with all creatures and with your heavenly Father–Mother.


# ALONE, YET NOT ALONE

When you come into the world of spirit you will notice in certain places complete silence and stillness. This is necessary for every soul.

Every soul must pass through the place of silence, the place of aloneness. Yet being alone, the soul is not alone.

## POWER IN THE SILENCE

In the silence there is power. When anxious, when the forces of the earth threaten to overrun the soul, in the silence will come endurance. In the silence will come the breaking of the light. Be silent and know God's power and God's love ... and deep soul peace.

# 15

ॐ

## BEING LIGHT-HEARTED:
## THE FINDING OF INNER JOY

*Many, many times White Eagle has spoken of how he and
those in spirit understand our sorrow and our pain; their
compassion and empathy is infinite. But, as a true spirit
brother, he demonstrates wise love by helping us to see how,
through our aspirations, thoughts and daily life, we can
still live joyously. Indeed, the whole of the teaching White
Eagle brings to us illumines a path of happiness which we
can tread—if we choose well and think rightly—with a
lightness of heart. Contact with, and aspiration towards,*

*the world of spirit, means a finding of that inner joy. And this inner joy and sense of fun, in their turn, are deeply healing, not just of the emotions, but of the body itself.*

## JOYOUS LOVE

Speak to another of that which lies in the heart, and be not ashamed of your words; for as you speak from your heart you are sounding notes of truth, wisdom and power. Do not be afraid of another person's opinion of you: give to the world the simplicity of a true and joyous love.

## THE INNER KNOWING

When truth comes into your heart you can smile. The wise among you never argue about truth. There is no need. You all experience this at times—you have that inner knowing. We do not mean a mental arrogance which is very sure of its cleverness, but that quiet, inner knowing, which never wants to argue. You can be quite still and quite happy.

## THE GIFT OF JOY

You are only one of a very vast family and every one of that family has to endure certain sorrows and pains, but also has the gift of enjoyment: enjoying life, enjoying the beauties of creation.

Think of this. Do not dwell on the endurance side of your life so much as on the enjoyment, the pleasures, the joy which God has given to all children on earth, the joy which completely outweighs the periods of stress and times of endurance.

## USE ME, O LORD

A humble spirit brings joy in living, in acceptance, in the knowledge that your Creator is with you. And if God, your Father and Mother, cannot use you in one way, they will use you in another, my child. 'Here I am, Lord: take me, and use me according to Thy will.'

## ENJOY FUN

Life is not solemn. Life is full of joy and fun … think of life as being eternal, and that you—a tiny spark of that divine life—are learning to walk a path which is leading you to union with your heavenly Parents. This is the goal of your life: conscious union with that divine love and peace and joy and—yes—fun. Jesus, when on earth, enjoyed fun!

## BE HAPPY

God does not want you to suffer or to be unhappy; but wants you to be happy and to know the Father–Mother and the divine power.

# THE SOURCE OF YOUR LIFE

God has placed you in this world to give you joy and happiness. Enjoy your life. Be happy and thankful for every glorious sensation which your body rightly gives to you. Enjoy every good gift of life, but never forget the Source of your life to which you owe everything.

## THE JOYFUL SPRING

Every son—daughter of the living God should live joyfully. In your own life, were you touching the secret of joy, if you had realized, if you had recognized, pure joy in your life, how different you would feel! Let us take for illustration the life of Jesus. If you knew in more detail the manner of his life, its simplicity, and his continual outpouring of the magical white light, you would understand what we mean when we say that joy and goodness are the spring which releases the power of the white magic—the spiritual life-force which is the core of all spiritual healing.

## HAPPINESS IS EVERYWHERE

Do not depend upon anyone else for your happiness, my dear ones; better to see it everywhere, shining like stars twinkling out of a deep blue sky at night. *In little things, in simple things, the Lord cometh.* God bringeth happiness and happiness is your birthright.

## THE GREAT AWAKENING

Every man and woman is crucified in matter; you yourselves are crucified when you suffer grievous pain and come up against harsh conditions: you truly are crucified. But will it help you if White Eagle tells you that when you are crucified you are very close to the great awakening; to the resurrection, when you will find greater beauty, more satisfying, deeper happiness, than you have ever known before?

## THE SECRET

This is the secret: to live, to know and to be, in the consciousness of the infinite love and light, and to live for spirit and not for matter. Matter is secondary; spirit is first and foremost in you, and to live rightly is to live to develop the consciousness of the Christ within yourself.